GINGERS

Kieran Dodds

First published in hardback by Hide Press in 2020.
This edition published by Hide Press in 2020.

Paintings on pp. 4 & 6 reproduced courtesy
of the National Galleries of Scotland.

Design by John McGill

Set in Akzidenz-Grotesk and Miller Display

Printed and bound in the Netherlands
by Wonderful Books, Eindhoven

ISBN 978-1-5272-8046-5

for Ada *and* Isobel

Introduction

There are, according to a dubious map on the Internet, two global hotspots for ginger hair. One is verified by science: Scotland. Some forty per cent of the residents in the country's capital, Edinburgh, are fortunate enough to carry at least one MC1R gene, the slice of biological coding that bestows red hair when two are present. Though in my homeland, only one in eight Scots are – like me – ginger, we are common enough to be something of a national cliché.

The other hotspot is less well documented, less famous, several thousand miles to the east. The city of Perm – a fitting name, really – lies on the Kama river upstream from the Udmurt Republic, an area known as the heart of the world's other great ginger enclave. When I was planning the trip there, my local assistant was sceptical of this fact until he was flooded with responses to a social-media post. On the walk to and from the studio, I continued to point out gingers until he admitted it was a thing. Against the grey buildings and sky their hair blazed like fires.

The Virgin Adoring the Sleeping Christ Child
Sandro Botticelli, c.1485

Tempera and gold on canvas, 122 × 80.3 cm

The National Galleries of Scotland, Edinburgh

And ginger looms large in imaginations far beyond its heartlands. There has been, to my knowledge, no census of hair colour in art, but ginger is ubiquitous on canvas and in oil. In Scotland's National Gallery in Edinburgh, every painting in the former Renaissance upper gallery had at least one ginger, with even more in works downstairs.

The glistering hair of Christ in Daddi's *Triptych* altarpiece; the golden halo-like locks of his mother Mary in the work of Botticelli; the amber waves flowing down upon Titian's Venus as she rises from the sea. 'Why so many gingers?' I asked a guide, and he laughed. Maybe it was simply because the works had been collected for a Scottish audience?

There are certainly plenty of local gingers in the Scottish National Portrait Gallery too, such as the eighteenth-century self-portrait of Edinburgh artist David Martin, which epitomises the inspiringly upfront and natural approach of Scottish enlightenment painters. While we can assume the depiction of his ginger self is accurate, the Renaissance subjects are rooted in antiquity and the Middle East, not Scotland.

I visited galleries in other cities, and the results of my informal survey were the same. It is so obvious: art abounds with gingers, and yet I had never noticed.

The works of past masters taught me two things that infused and inspired this series. Firstly, they show us that ginger is a universal characteristic, stretching way beyond a mere Celtic fringe. My subjects bear that point out: a Scottish boy with an Eastern European mother and a Middle Eastern father (p.13) or even an Indian grandfather (pp. 29 & 81); a Russian woman with a Chinese paternal line (p.89); the famed 'Red People' of Treasure Beach, Jamaica, where surnames speak not just of Scottish heritage but also of English, French and Asian ancestry.

And secondly, the depiction of ginger in art reminds us how artists use colour and light to draw attention to their subject. We may not directly admire the sunlight on a pot of gold, but it can make a treasure more dazzling – or more dreadful, depending on who covets it. Jesus' hair may not have been ginger, for example, but its vibrancy in paintings draws our eyes to him. We cannot, of course, surmise from this that ginger hair is somehow divine, nor, for that matter, devilish, as others might say. But the splendour of this colour, and its rarity, has dazzled humanity through the centuries, lifting our eyes beyond the dull and drab.

Gingers transects eleven time zones, from the Americas through Europe, on to the Middle East and Asia. The people who bear the genes, who carry the hair, have unique histories. They occupy different political regions. But they are united by a golden – well, coppery, or rusty, as the Russians would say – thread: the flow of DNA across cultures and generations, a reminder that all people are made of the same substance, and sometimes it shows.

Kieran Dodds

◀ **Self-portrait**
David Martin, 1760

Oil on canvas,
49.5 × 39.4 cm

The National Galleries
of Scotland, Edinburgh

THE PORTRAITS

► **Caitlin & Abigail Young**
Scotland
b. 2012

▶ **Alexander Soued**
Scotland
b. 2011

◀◀ **Zlata Imennych**
Russia
b. 1996

◀ **Gilad Belkin**
Israel
b. 1988

▶ **Nixie Connelly**
Scotland
b. 2014

▶ **Jordan DeLeon**
Jamaica
b. 2016

▶ **Steven Mackay**
Scotland
b. 1976

▶ **Esther Mackay**
Scotland
b. 2012

▶ **Rebecca Mackay**
Scotland
b. 1981

▶ **Chloe Mackay**
Scotland
b. 2006

▶ **Lois Mackay**
Scotland
b. 2008

▶ **Abigail Mackay**
Scotland
b. 2010

◀ **Tatiana & Valeria Korotaeva**
Russia
b. 1998 & 1999

▸ **John Ross**
Scotland
b. 1950

▶ **Hannah Warren**
Scotland
b. 2001

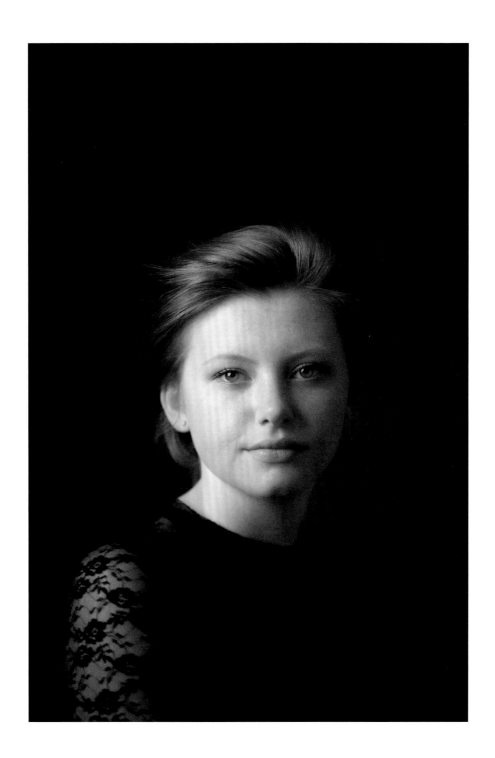

▶ **Josh Hallam**
Scotland
b. 2005

▶ **Natasha McDonald**
Scotland
b. 2006

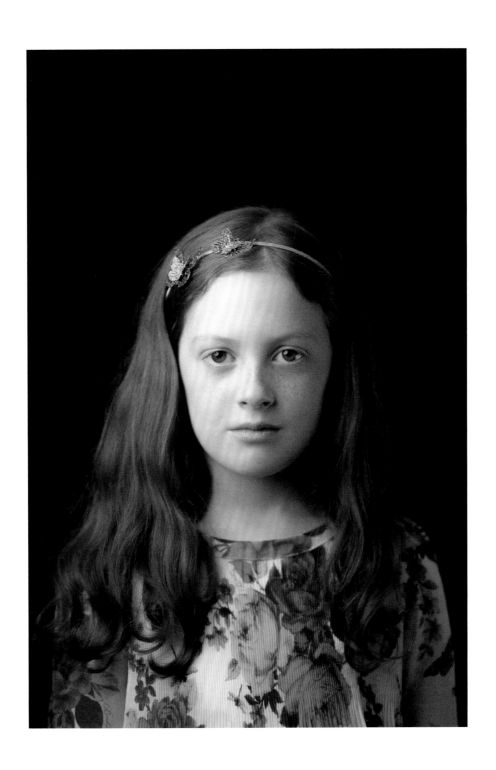

▶ **James Buswell**
England
b.1988

▶ **Mark Mordey**
England
b.1951

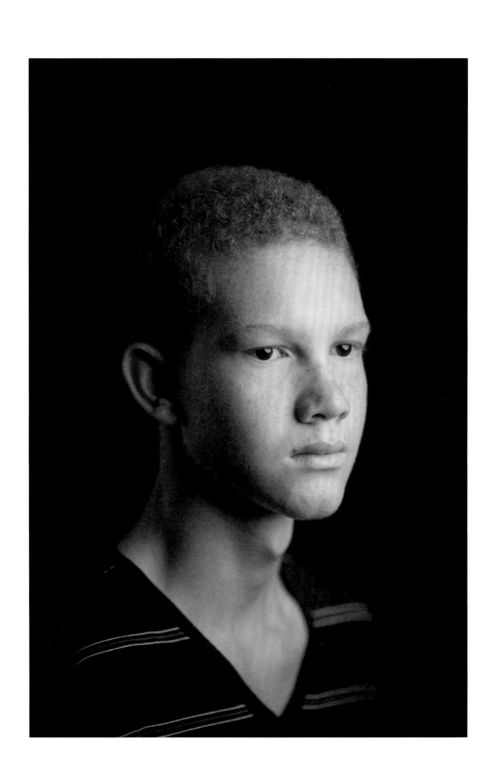

◀ **Leon Swaby**
Jamaica
b. 2004

▶ **Victoria Sergiyenko**
Russia
b. 2008

▶ **Anna Dodds**
Scotland
b. 2010

► **Ceara McVey**
Scotland
b. 1999

◀◀ **Mariya Suhoeva**
Russia
b. 1996

◀ **Max Shetenicok**
Russia
b. 1984

▶ **Artem Oznobishin**
Russia
b. 1992

▶ **Chris McCabe**
Scotland
b. 1991

◀ **Wasim Lloyd**
Jamaica
b. 1996

▶ **Esther Mackay**
Scotland
b. 2012

▶ **Becky Jeffcoates**
England
b. 1972

▶ **Marlyn Cameron**
Scotland
b. 1945

◀◀ **Anna Vechtomova**
Russia
b. 1982

◀ **Roy Brian**
Scotland
b. 1976

▶ **Madison McCready**
Scotland
b. 2015

▶ **Marcos Rodriguez De Abreu**
England
b. 2008

◀ **Phil Ford**
Scotland
b. 1981

▶ **Jack McNaughton**
Scotland
b. 2007

▸ **Rianne Wouda**
Netherlands
b. 1990

▶ **Caitlin Greene**
Scotland
b. 2006

▶ **Dez Johnston**
Scotland
b. 1982

▶ **Regina Vaganova**
Russia
b.1996

▶ **Lucy Fleming**
Scotland
b. 2005

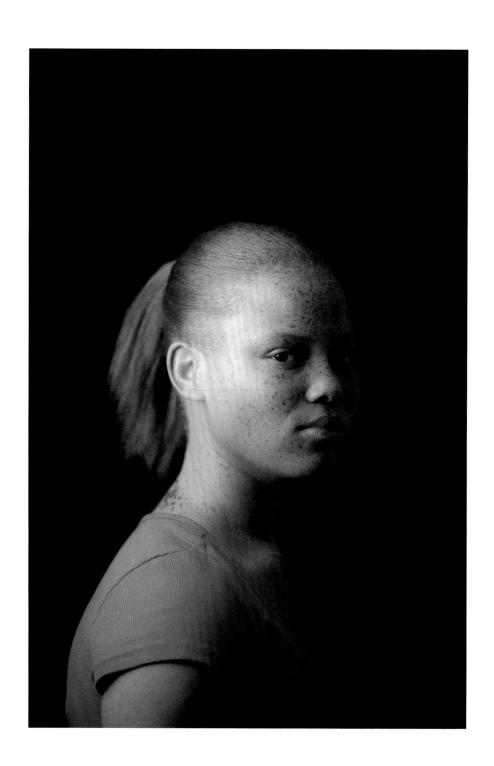

◀ **Marteka Nembhard**
Jamaica
b. 2005

▶ **Jamie Hallam**
Scotland
b. 2004

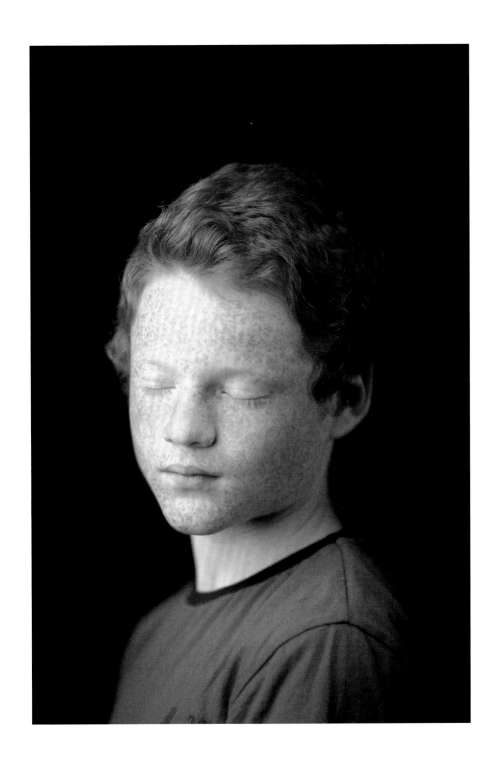

▶ **Colin Cummings**
Scotland
b. 1981

▶ **Egor Potapov & daughter**
Russia
b. 1983 & 2017

▶ **Dasha Shipitcina**
Russia
b.1994

◀◀ **Nikolaj Loufbye**
Denmark
b. 1993

◀ **Sveta Ni**
Russia
b. 1996

▶ **Bridget James**
Jamaica
b. 1996

◀ **Pacey Young**
Scotland
b. 2002

▶ **Are Ginzburg**
Russia
b. 2013

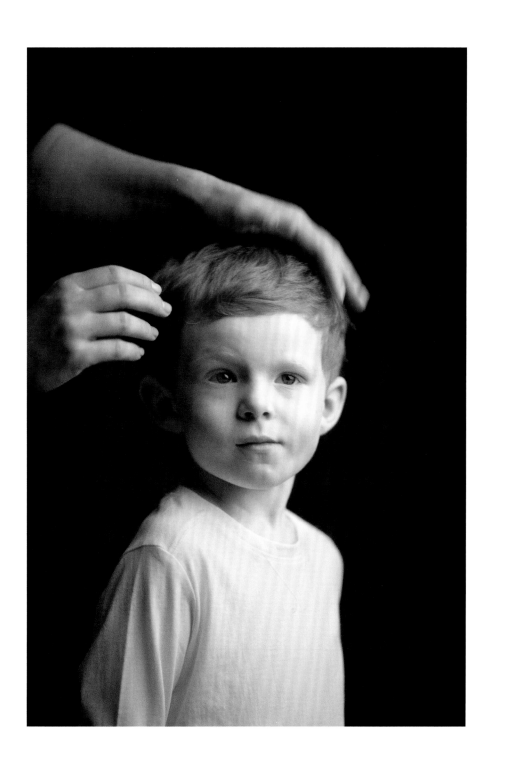

▶ **Jennifer Hutchison & Finn Arnold**
Scotland
b. 1986 & 2016

▶ **Maya Duncan-Smith**
Scotland
b. 2008

◀◀ **Igor Ferdinand Von Sell**
Russia
b. 1993

◀ **Asya Alypova**
Russia
b. 1989

▶ **Artem Loginov**
Russia
b. 2000

▶ **Lynn Ballingall**
Scotland
b. 1992

◀ **Elena Adrian**
Russia
b. 2005

▶ **Stewart Black**
Scotland
b. 2005

▶ **Duncan Magill**
Scotland
b. 1997

▸ **Thomas Brown**
Scotland
b. 1989

▶ **Elizavet Bystrykh**
Russia
b. 2014

▶ **Faye Tudor**
Scotland
b. 1979

▶ **Caitlin Palmer**
Scotland
b. 1994

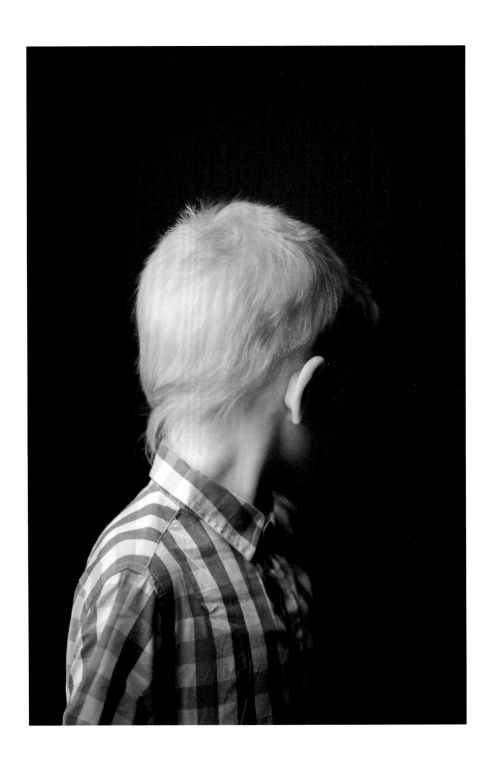

◀ **Nikolay Bystrykh**
Russia
b. 2011

▶ **Randy Wong**
Jamaica
b. 1988

▶ **Anna Ustalova**
Russia
b. 2008

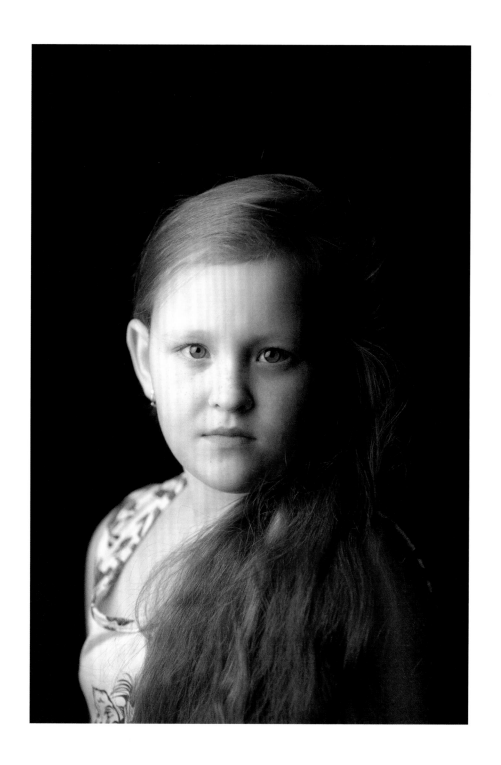

▶ **Pauline Huguet**
France
b. 1993

▸ **Kieran Dodds**
Scotland
b.1980

▸ **Mariya Scorohodova**
Russia
b.1994

▶ **Margarita Bezukladnikova**
Russia
b. 2013

◀ **Isobel & Ada Dodds**
Scotland
b. 2016

The photographer

Kieran Dodds is known internationally for portraits and photo stories that examine the interplay of environment and culture. He lives in Edinburgh, Scotland with his wife and twin daughters.

The people behind the pictures

Behind each photograph there is a host of people to thank – most obviously the people who were willing to be photographed for this series, some of whom appear in this book.

Those who supported me personally, including my Mum and Dad, who also provided the ginger genes. Caz, who encouraged me to pursue the story even when it meant leaving her with the kids while I escaped to a Jamaican paradise.

Those who helped create the work, especially first assistant Lynn Ballingall (p.105) for proving the concept.

Overseas assistants who became friends: Ilias Farkhutdinov in Perm, Russia, and Rowena Powell in Treasure Beach, Jamaica.

Those who made the work visible: Adrian and the brilliant Panos Pictures family, who patiently listen to all my ramblings. Fiona Shields at *The Guardian* for publishing the work across the years. Alistair Gordon and David McCulloch of Morphé Arts for exhibitions in Dundee and London. Matt Sillars at the Flow Photofest in Inverness for showing the British and Russian *Gingers* side by side, and Olga Emelianova of Mediacongress for taking them to join historic cousins in the State Hermitage, St Petersburg.

Scientific advice from Professor Jonathan Rees and Professor Ian Jackson has been foundational and invaluable.

For the book: thanks to Marc Prust for providing clarity, Niall McDiarmid for inspiration, John McGill for making years of work into a tangible thing, Rory Smith for helping me put into words what I want to say and Sarah Ream for sharpening my thoughts and the text.

Finally, to all gingers: thank you for making our world a brighter place.